FIT TO FOLLOW

A Study of Discipleship

Bible Crossroads

Bible Way CRC Publications
Grand Rapids, Michigan

Acknowledgments

The Education Department is grateful to Dan Vander Ark for writing this course in the *Bible Crossroads* series. Dan is a professional teacher and the principal of Holland Christian High School, Holland, Michigan.

We are also grateful to Paul Stoub, free-lance artist from Grand Rapids, Michigan, for designing and illustrating this textbook.

The Scripture quotations in this publication are from the HOLY BIBLE, NEW INTERNATIONAL VERSION. Copyright © 1973, 1978, 1984 International Bible Society. Used by permission of Zondervan Bible Publishers.

Copyright © 1989 by CRC Publications, 2850 Kalamazoo SE, Grand Rapids, Michigan 49560.

All rights reserved. With the exception of brief excerpts for review purposes, no part of this book may be reproduced in any manner whatsoever without written permission from the publisher. Printed in the United States of America on recycled paper. ♻

5 4 3

ISBN 0-930265-77-7

Contents

Lesson 1	Lord, Call Our Names	4
Lesson 2	Lord, Give Us Faith	12
Lesson 3	Lord, Help Us Listen	20
Lesson 4	Lord, Teach Us to Pray	26
Lesson 5	Lord, Help Us to Care	32
Lesson 6	Lord, Make Us More Like You	40
Lesson 7	Lord, Make Us Forgiving	46
Lesson 8	Lord, Discipline Our Lives	54
Lesson 9	Lord, Give Us Courage	62
Lesson 10	Lord, Accept Our Thanks	68
Lesson 11	Lord, Help Us Grow	76
Lesson 12	Lord, Help Us Witness	84

Take-Home Sheets 91

Todd was a wimp. Kids picked on him, teased him, and beat him up. Todd always felt frightened. But even though he was skinny and scared, he always tried to fight back. Unfortunately, he was the only person who ended up with a bruised body and bruised feelings. He was sick of it. Then he met Willis, a strange old man. As they talked, Todd discovered that Willis knew karate. Todd begged Willis to teach him the ancient art. Willis's ways were strange, but the two worked together for weeks and months. And even though Todd often felt like quitting, he didn't. He followed Willis—even when Willis asked him to do weird things. Finally Todd, the wimp, knew karate well enough to meet—and beat—his tormenters. But even though the bullies quit bothering him, Todd still followed his strange old friend.

The little girl in the home movie rocked her doll gently, kissing its little nose and cooing soft nothings in its ear—just like Mommy did with her baby sister. Then the little girl put a tiny aluminum pot on her toy stove. With her dolly in one arm, she carefully stirred the "soup" with her other hand—just like Mommy used to do.

Everyone watching the movie burst into amused laughter at the little girl's comic antics that were recorded years ago. Today Sherry, the little girl, is twenty-two and about to be married. Her family is gathering to celebrate and reminisce. Sherry laughed until tears rolled down her cheeks. "Hey, that's just the way you did it, Mom. I was trying to imitate you. I can't believe it!"

Eric hated the fact that his parents signed him up for piano lessons. Why couldn't he just play hockey like the other guys? He liked music, but this was *too much* music.

But as the lessons progressed, he found himself spending more time at the piano. Each new piece was a challenge; the hours passed quickly as he strove for perfection. When he finally got a piece right, it was fun—he felt really good. And the better Eric played, the more excited his teacher became. "I

Lo

LESSON 1

Almost all of us look up to and follow someone. Why? Perhaps that someone is wiser than we are. Maybe that someone acts the way we'd like to act—but can't. Maybe that someone has a skill we'd like to have: athletic ability, a talent for singing or drawing, a quick mathematical mind. Maybe that someone is really friendly and we wish we could be nicer to others.

When we choose to follow someone, we pay for it—sometimes with time, money, interest, or even our freedom. But we also gain something—a new knowledge that will help us in the future, a friendship that makes us feel valuable, or the excitement of getting someplace we wouldn't have been able to go without the help of this master teacher.

In this course you'll learn what it means to choose to follow Jesus, the greatest teacher ever. Jesus' very first followers were plain people; he called them disciples. These simple followers readily trusted Jesus and eagerly followed him. They didn't hold back! The lessons in this book will show you what it means to follow the Lord in the same way that the disciples did.

know you can play even better. But you must follow my plan for you!" his teacher had said at his last lesson. Then she had shown him exactly how to play an even more impossible piece. Eric sensed that she knew all he needed to learn about playing the piano. So he listened, practiced, and followed her every word.

d, Call Our Names

Matthew 9:9–13

Name:
Matthew (means "gift of the Lord")

Occupation:
tax collector for the Roman government, probably a tollbooth operator on the main road between Damascus and Israel

Income Bracket:
upper-middle class (makes a good living by honest and dishonest means—overcharges by 20 percent and pockets the difference for himself)

Social Standing:
low, a social outcast (considered a traitor by fellow Jews because he works for the hated Romans; called a swindler because he cheats his own people by overcharging them)

⁹As Jesus went on from there, he saw a man named Matthew sitting at the tax collector's booth. "Follow me," he told him, and Matthew got up and followed him. ¹⁰While Jesus was having dinner at Matthew's house, many tax collectors and "sinners" came and ate with him and his disciples. ¹¹When the Pharisees saw this, they asked his disciples, "Why does your teacher eat with tax collectors and 'sinners'?" ¹²On hearing this, Jesus said, "It is not the healthy who need a doctor, but the sick. ¹³But go and learn what this means: 'I desire mercy, not sacrifice.' For I have not come to call the righteous, but sinners."

Discuss/Decide

1. Underline the words Jesus used to invite Matthew to be his disciple. How does Jesus invite us to follow him today?

2. How did Matthew respond to Jesus' call to follow him? How does Jesus want us to respond to his invitation to follow him?

3. What did the Pharisees think of Jesus' choice of disciples and friends? What do you think Jesus meant by his answer to their question "Why does your teacher eat with tax collectors and 'sinners' ?"

4. In Matthew 11:28–30 Jesus makes a promise to all who obediently respond to the call to follow him. What is that promise? How does Jesus' invitation and promise make you feel?

Yes, but...

"I'm not good enough to follow Jesus."

"I don't need to follow anyone—I can handle my own problems!"

"I'm not even sure whether Jesus is calling me."

"I need to be a little older."

"Won't following Jesus mean I will have to give up my fun?"

"I'll probably mess up . . . I don't think I can handle it."

Litany of Commitment

Leader: Jesus said "Come, follow me . . . and I will make you fishers of men" (Matt. 4:19).

Group: We will follow you.

Leader: Jesus said, "Come to me, all you who are weary and burdened, and I will give you rest" (Matt. 11:28).

Group: We will follow you.

Leader: Jesus said, "He who sent me is reliable, and what I have heard from him I tell the world" (John 8:26b).

Group: We will learn from you.

Leader: Jesus said, "If you hold to my teaching, you are really my disciples. Then you will know the truth, and the truth will set you free" (John 8:31b–32).

Group: We want to be your disciples.

Leader: Jesus said, "I tell you the truth, he who believes has everlasting life" (John 6:47).

Group: Lord, we will follow you.

Think About It . . .

If Jesus appeared in person tomorrow, where do you think you would find him?

Lord, Give Us Faith

Everywhere Jesus went, people followed. They came to hear him, learn from him, and receive his healing. Long days with pressing crowds tired the Master; he needed time with his small group of disciples. More than that, he needed time alone.

LESSON 2

At the end of an extremely busy day, Jesus sent his disciples on ahead, asking them to go by boat to the other side of the Sea of Galilee. He would meet them there later.

Then Jesus climbed the hillside. Alone at last. But for Jesus, being alone meant spending time with God, a time to pray and to receive strength to continue his ministry.

Meanwhile, a fierce storm was brewing on the sea of Galilee. Violent winds beat against the small boat. Inside, the terrified disciples huddled together, hoping the storm would end quickly. But it only became worse.

The storm raged throughout the night. Toward morning, the frightened disciples spotted something—or someone—approaching their boat through the darkness. A person? No, it must be a ghost!

Jesus' voice came over the roaring wind and waves, calming the disciples' fright and reminding them of his love and power. Jesus told them to take courage.

Peter, filled with new courage and love for his Lord, was eager to show Jesus his faith. He was ready to walk over the waves to meet his master. Jesus told him to walk toward him.

As the disciples watched fearfully, Peter walked on the waves to meet Jesus. But, as Peter glanced around, feeling the wind catch his clothes, his courage vanished; his trust in Jesus wobbled. Peter began to slip beneath the water! He cried out to Jesus to save him.

Peter immediately felt Jesus' hand reach out to grab his. Peter also heard the disappointment in Jesus' voice. Jesus told Peter he was a man of little faith.

Peter noticed the winds calm and the waves smooth out as Jesus climbed into the boat with him. Peter wondered how he could have forgotten to trust his Lord so quickly.

The rest of the disciples shared Peter's thoughts. With Peter, they knelt down right there in the boat and worshiped Jesus.

1. What do the first three frames tell you about Jesus, the Master? Why do you think Matthew, the biblical storyteller, includes this detail about Jesus?

2. Based on this story from the gospel of Matthew, describe Peter as a person. Describe Peter's faith in Jesus.

3. Circle the words that show Jesus' reaction when Peter began to falter and slip beneath the waves. How would Jesus define the kind of faith he expects from his disciples? Write a definition of that kind of faith in your own words.

4. How did the disciples respond to Jesus when all were safe in the boat and the wind had quieted? When, if ever, have you felt the same way about Jesus?

5. Give some examples from your own life (or from the lives of Christians you know) that illustrate how Jesus tests the faith of his disciples today.

Discuss/Decide

Worry Survey

Everyone has a fear or worry. What are you afraid of? What worries you? Jesus also knows that his followers have fears (check out his words to us in today's memory work). Look at the following list of common fears and worries today's young people often have. Mark the fears and worries that might take *your* eyes off Jesus and cause your faith to wobble.

I worry that . . .

	HARDLY AT ALL	SOMETIMES	OFTEN
my friends will reject me			
my parents will die			
nuclear war might break out			
my grades will drop			
I'll get involved with drugs and alcohol			
someone I love will get a terminal disease			
I won't be able to buy new clothes			
my parents will get divorced			
my friends will get me in trouble			
kids at school will pick on me			
I'll die young			
other:			
other:			

What a Friend We Have in Jesus

1. What a friend we have in Jesus, all our sins and griefs to bear!
What a privilege to carry everything to God in prayer!
Oh, what peace we often forfeit, oh, what needless pain we bear,
all because we do not carry everything to God in prayer.

2. Have we trials and temptations? Is there trouble anywhere?
We should never be discouraged; take it to the Lord in prayer.
Can we find a friend so faithful, who will all our sorrows share?
Jesus knows our every weakness; take it to the Lord in prayer.

3. Are we weak and heavy laden, cumbered with a load of care?
Precious Savior, still our refuge! Take it to the Lord in prayer.
Do your friends despise, forsake you? Take it to the Lord in prayer!
In his arms he'll take and shield you; you will find a solace there.

Text: Joseph M. Scriven, 1855
Tune: The Sacred Harp, Philadelphia, 1844; harm. A. Royce Eckhardt, 1972.
Harmonization © 1972, Covenant Press

Think About It...

Imagine how you would feel if you asked your best friend what he or she thinks of you and your friend said, "You're nice and fun to be with; I could spend hours talking to you, but sometimes I don't quite trust you." How do you think Jesus feels when his followers act as if they don't really trust him or believe his promises?

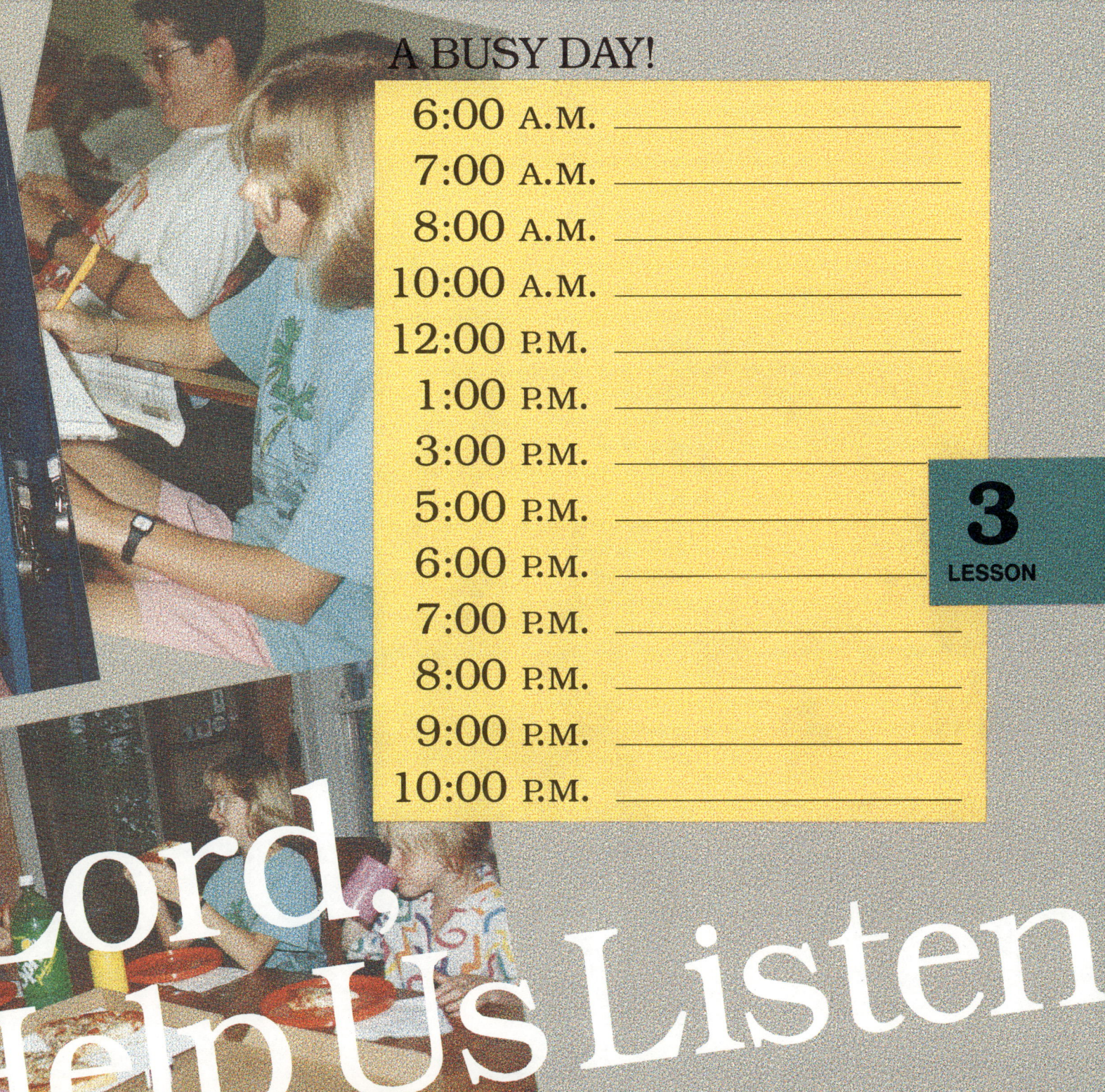

A BUSY DAY!

6:00 A.M. _____
7:00 A.M. _____
8:00 A.M. _____
10:00 A.M. _____
12:00 P.M. _____
1:00 P.M. _____
3:00 P.M. _____
5:00 P.M. _____
6:00 P.M. _____
7:00 P.M. _____
8:00 P.M. _____
9:00 P.M. _____
10:00 P.M. _____

LESSON 3

Lord, Help Us Listen

Luke 10:38–42

Discuss/Decide

⁳⁸As Jesus and his disciples were on their way, he came to a village where a woman named Martha opened her home to him. ³⁹She had a sister called Mary, who sat at the Lord's feet listening to what he said. ⁴⁰But Martha was distracted by all the preparations that had to be made. She came to him and asked, "Lord, don't you care that my sister has left me to do the work by myself? Tell her to help me!"

⁴¹"Martha, Martha," the Lord answered, "you are worried and upset about many things, ⁴²but only one thing is needed. Mary has chosen what is better, and it will not be taken away from her."

1. What does Martha's invitation to Jesus and his disciples tell you about the kind of person she was?

_____

2. What does Martha's comment to Jesus (v. 40) suggest about how she viewed her time and service to Jesus?

_____

3. What does Jesus' answer to Martha say about what is the most important way disciples of Jesus can use their time?

_____

4. What does this story have to say to followers of Jesus today? What does it mean for us today to sit at Jesus' feet or to take time to listen to him?

_____

5. In what ways does listening to Jesus help us become better disciples, ready to serve him? (Check 2 Timothy 3:16–17.)

_____

6. List some common distractions that can keep us from taking time each day to listen to Jesus.

Lord, Help Us Listen

Lord, I'm so busy every day with _____
_____
_____

I want to take time to listen to you because _____
_____
_____

The part of your Word that I'd like to learn more about is _____
_____
_____

I would like to take _____ minutes each day to listen to your Word and to learn more about you. The best time of day for me is _____
_____

Lord, help me listen!

FEAST

Mary,
contrary
to men's
expectations,
your priority
was not to set
the supper table
or to fix
the food
though you were well
acquainted with both.

The best dish
of the evening
was to sit
and listen
and learn
and take a part
in the delicious
conversation.

You chose the better portion.

(Taken from *Beginning with Mary: Women of the Gospels in Portrait* by Thomas John Carlisle, Grand Rapids: Eerdmans, 1986, p. 80. Used by permission of the publisher.)

Think About It . . .

Martin Luther once said, "I have so much business I cannot get on without spending three hours daily in prayer." Is that how it usually works with Jesus' disciples? Or is the opposite true? Which one are you—Martha or Martin?

■ "I love to come to your house to be with you; I wish I could live in your house."

■ "Check me out; discover if I'm really sincere about liking you. Please keep me from being influenced by bad peer pressure. Sometimes it's tricky."

■ "Hey, remember me? Seems like you're ignoring me. How much longer do I have to put up with my messed up mind?"

■ "Please forgive me? I've really blown it. Every time I close my eyes, all I can see is how I've offended you."

■ "Wow! That's really beautiful! A masterpiece—perfectly put together! You pay attention to every detail; what tender, loving care."

■ "Whenever I get scared, I know I can count on you. I trust you so much that I'm not even worried when my so-called friends try to mess me up."

■ "You know what's on my mind today? The poor. They get picked on all the time; nobody stands up for them. Please help, will you?"

Suppose all these statements were said by the same person to a certain individual. What do these statements show about the speaker? About the person he or she is addressing? What can you conclude about the relationship between the speaker and listener?

Prayer is _____
_____

Disciples' prayers include

1. _____
2. _____
3. _____

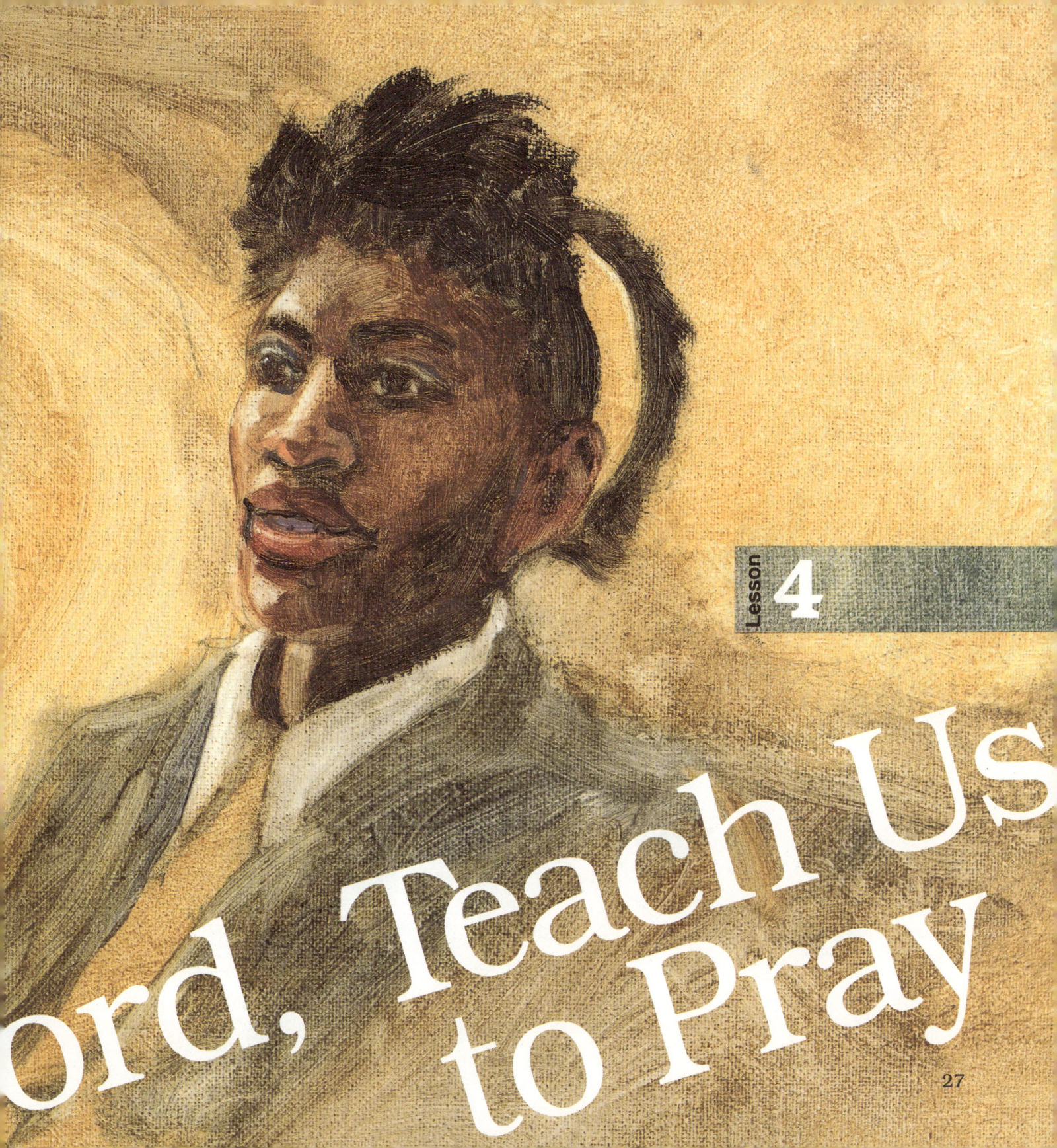

Matthew 6:5–15

⁵And when you pray, do not be like the hypocrites, for they love to pray standing in the synagogues and on the street corners to be seen by men. I tell you the truth, they have received their reward in full. ⁶But when you pray, go into your room, close the door and pray to your Father, who is unseen. Then your Father, who sees what is done in secret, will reward you. ⁷And when you pray, do not keep on babbling like pagans, for they think they will be heard because of their many words. ⁸Do not be like them, for your Father knows what you need before you ask him.

⁹This, then, is how you should pray:

"Our Father in heaven,
hallowed be your name,
¹⁰your kingdom come,
your will be done
on earth as it is in heaven.
¹¹Give us today our daily bread.
¹²Forgive us our debts,
as we also have forgiven our debtors.
¹³And lead us not into temptation,
but deliver us from the evil one."

¹⁴For if you forgive men when they sin against you, your heavenly Father will also forgive you. ¹⁵But if you do not forgive men their sins, your Father will not forgive your sins.

1. Jesus uses this passage to teach us how and how not to pray. What does Jesus call people who pray publicly for the wrong reasons? What is their motivation for praying the way they do?

2. From the passage, draw as many conclusions as you can about how we *should* pray.

3. Read the Lord's Prayer as it is found in verses 9–13. Divide the prayer into two distinct sections and list the three requests in each section. What is the emphasis of the first section? The second section?

4. Why is prayer necessary for Jesus' disciples if their needs are already known to him (see v. 8)?

5. First Thessalonians 5:16–18 has this advice for disciples of Jesus: "Be joyful always; pray continually; give thanks in all circumstances. . . ." What do you think it means to pray continually?

Discuss/Decide

Father, We Love You

Q. How does God want us to pray so that he will listen to us?

A. First, we must pray from the heart
  to no other than the one true God,
  who has revealed himself in his Word,
  asking for everything he has commanded us to ask for.

Second, we must acknowledge our need and misery,
  hiding nothing,
  and humble ourselves in his majestic presence.

Third, we must rest on this unshakable foundation:
  even though we do not deserve it,
  God will surely listen to our prayer
  because of Christ our Lord.
  That is what he promised us in his Word.

Heidelberg Catechism Q & A 117

Q. What did God command us to pray for?

A. Everything we need, spiritually and physically,
  as embraced in the prayer Christ our Lord himself taught us.

Heidelberg Catechism Q & A 118

1 Father,
2 Jesus, we love you, we worship, we adore you,
3 Spirit,

glorify your name in all the earth,
glorify your name, glorify your name,
glorify your name in all the earth.

Text and Tune: Donna Adkins, 1976; harm. Dale Grotenhuis, 1985. © 1976, 1981, Maranatha! Music c/o The Copyright Company, Nashville, TN. All rights reserved. International copyright secured. Used by permission.

Gus-Gus Has Fleas

Today I learned that "Gus-Gus" is dead.

"Gus-Gus" wasn't her real name. It was a thoughtless nickname the boys of Goldfield Junior High School gave to a skinny, dark-visaged little girl whose real name was Barbara.

Why we called her "Gus-Gus," I really don't know. Maybe we thought she resembled the wharf rat in the Disney pictures. Whatever the reason, I think we treated the rats in our biology class with more respect than we did Barbara.

Somehow we got into the game of running up and touching her and then tossing her "fleas" when the bell rang. Otherwise you were stuck with them until the next bell. If that happened, we would grimace and groan as we manfully bore our burden. We never thought of her burden.

To us it was funny.

Then.

Not now. Now that I'm older and wiser. Now that I'm sober and sorry. Now that I've learned "Gus-Gus" is dead—killed outright in a grinding car-train collision a few years back.

At the Class of 1964 Reunion, where I learned of

Lord, Help Us to Care

LESSON 5

Barbara's untimely death, another classmate and I were talking about the good times we used to have in school. And we did have good times! But we both agreed that if we had a chance to do it all over again, we would cut out that stupid little "flea game."

We can see now that it wasn't a game to Barbara. How many times did that poor girl have her feelings hurt and spirit crushed by our crude antics? Only God knows. And since God knows, I must tell *Him* I'm sorry. Because I can't tell Barbara now.

One particular day, the teasing got so bad that she became physically sick and threw up at her desk. I can see her—head down, tears splashing the varnished finish of the desk, eyes like a wounded deer, frail body shaking.

I also remember the day Barbara and her family moved from our little Iowa community. The school principal, Mr. Jones, stormed into our home room and chewed us out for the way we had dehumanized Barbara.

We were sophomores at the time. Our heartless entertainment hadn't ended with the passing of junior high days, and Mr. Jones made us feel about two inches tall. We deserved every word of the overdue tongue-lashing we received that day.

But what could we have done then? She had moved away. What can we do now? She is dead.

If you've ever hurt or sinned against someone whose whereabouts are unknown, or if that person is dead, what can you do? There is only one thing.

Since people are made in the image and likeness of our Savior-Creator (Gen. 1:27), you can confess your sins to him. You might regret what you said or did to someone long ago, but you won't regret asking God's forgiveness.

Be sorry for hurting his creation—human life. There is healing power in repentance.

I know.

(Taken from "Gus-Gus Has Fleas" by Victor Knowles, September, 1982. This article originally appeared in *Moody Monthly*.)

Matthew 15:29–39

²⁹Jesus left there and went along the Sea of Galilee. Then he went up on a mountainside and sat down. ³⁰Great crowds came to him, bringing the lame, the blind, the crippled, the mute and many others, and laid them at his feet; and he healed them. ³¹The people were amazed when they saw the mute speaking, the crippled made well, the lame walking and the blind seeing. And they praised the God of Israel.

³²Jesus called his disciples to him and said, "I have compassion for these people; they have already been with me three days and have nothing to eat. I do not want to send them away hungry, or they may collapse on the way."

³³His disciples answered, "Where could we get enough bread in this remote place to feed such a crowd?"

³⁴How many loaves do you have?" Jesus asked.

"Seven," they replied, "and a few small fish."

³⁵He told the crowd to sit down on the ground. ³⁶Then he took the seven loaves and the fish, and when he had given thanks, he broke them and gave them to the disciples, and they in turn to the people. ³⁷They all ate and were satisfied. Afterward the disciples picked up seven basketfuls of broken pieces that were left over. ³⁸The number of those who ate was four thousand, besides women and children. ³⁹After Jesus had sent the crowd away, he got into the boat and went to the vicinity of Magadan.

Matthew 25:35–40

³⁵For I was hungry and you gave me something to eat, I was thirsty and you gave me something to drink, I was a stranger and you invited me in, ³⁶I needed clothes and you clothed me, I was sick and you looked after me, I was in prison and you came to visit me.

³⁷Then the righteous will answer him, "Lord, when did we see you hungry and feed you, or thirsty and give you something to drink? ³⁸When did we see you a stranger and invite you in, or needing clothes and clothe you? ³⁹When did we see you sick or in prison and go to visit you?"

⁴⁰The King will reply, "I tell you the truth, whatever you did for one of the least of these brothers of mine, you did for me."

1. Describe yourself in a sentence or two and tell why you joined the crowd around Jesus.

2. What was your first reaction when you saw Jesus heal people who had never walked or talked before? Did you express your feelings to anyone around you? If so, what did you say?

3. From your experience as a member of the crowd, would you say Jesus had empathy for others? Would you describe him as compassionate? Give some reasons for your answers.

4. When did you first feel hungry? How did you feel as you watched Jesus break bread and feed the people around you?

5. How has it helped you to watch Jesus and feel his compassion for people? How has it changed the way you reach out to others?

6. (*The following question is optional.*) Describe with imagination and detail another time and place when you observed Jesus' empathy and compassion for someone (or yourself). What did Jesus say or do to demonstrate his compassion? (You'll need a Bible for this. Here are some passages to activate your imagination: Matthew 8:5–13; 9:18–26; 20:29–34; Mark 1:40–45; 6:45–52; 10:13–16; Luke 7:11–17; John 11:17–44; 19:25–27.)

FOR PERSONAL REFLECTION . . .

Read Matthew 25:35–40. Is Jesus talking to you?

Exercising Empathy

The first part of compassion is empathy—the ability to feel someone else's feelings, to understand that person so well you can almost walk in his shoes. Remember the old Indian proverb? "You can't really talk with a person until you've walked a mile in his moccasins." Well, that's empathy! Close your eyes and walk a mile in the shoes of someone who was

- chosen last for a team at school.
- called a nasty nickname by classmates
- ridiculed for her clothes.
- left out of party plans because of a handicap.

Got the feeling? Then you've got empathy.

But compassion is *more* than empathy; it's doing something with that feeling (remember "Gus-Gus"?). Once you feel someone else's need or hurt, you have to make a choice. Showing compassion means making the choice to reach out and help that person.

After thinking about the situations described on the next page, do the following:

1. Exercise empathy. Decide who needs help and how that person is feeling.

2. Make a compassionate choice. Describe how you might reach out and help in a caring way.

Cultivating Compassion

It's Friday night and you're ready to go to the basketball game at the high school. All your friends will be there. While your family is at the supper table, the phone rings. Your grandpa has just been admitted to the hospital and he's asking you to come with your mom and dad to be with him tonight.

It's 6:00 A.M. and you're awake just enough to notice the huge snow drifts outside your window. The tree branches are bending under the heavy snow. You want to snuggle under your cozy blankets for another half hour, but your family has promised to shovel your invalid neighbor's walk this winter. It's your turn.

As you are walking down the hall with your friends, making plans to play softball during noon hour, your math teacher catches your eye and motions you over. She asks you if you would mind spending fifteen minutes of your lunch hour with Sherri, a new student who needs some help in catching up on her math.

Someone I would like to have more empathy for is:
But these things keep getting in my way:

1.

2.

Before this week is over, I am going to show more compassion by

Lord, Make Us More Like You

LESSON 6

The Associated Press

SAN PEDRO CUTUD, Philippines—At least 11 people were nailed to crosses and thousands of Filipinos beat their backs bloody today as the only Christian nation in Asia commemorated the crucifixion and death of Jesus Christ.

About 5,000 people, including foreign tourists and U.S. servicemen from nearby Clark Air Base, gathered on a rice field to watch men dressed as Roman centurions hammer nails into the palms and feet of Mario Castro and six other "Christs."

The crucifixions have been an annual ritual for decades in this village 40 miles north of Manila.

At the village entrance, the Department of Tourism posted a sign saying "Fiesta Islands," the theme of its current campaign to attract foreign tourists to the economically pressed country.

This year, the spectacle attracted seven "Christs," all voluntarily performing the ritual of having themselves nailed for reasons ranging from atonement for sins and thanksgiving for favors to requests for a bright future.

In Kapitangan in neighboring Bulacan province, Luciana Reyes, 30, had her palms and feet nailed to a wooden cross for the 13th straight year.

Another woman was also to have been crucified, but she screamed in pain when the nails pierced her palms and the ritual was discontinued.

At least two more crucifixions were reported in Iloces Norte province and one in Bataan, but details were not available because of poor communication lines.

To prevent infection, alcohol is poured on the crucifixion wounds and sterile gauze is applied.

The nails are stainless steel, extremely sharp and slender and are kept in alcohol. Through years of practice, the "centurions" who hammer the nails have learned where to drive the nails to avoid hitting bones. To ensure the smallest possible wound, only one hammer blow is delivered to each nail.

("Eleven Filipinos crucified in Good Friday reenactments," *The Grand Rapids Press*, March 24, 1989. Used by permission of Associated Press Newsfeatures.)

Colossians 2:6–7

⁶So then, just as you received Christ Jesus as Lord, continue to live in him, ⁷rooted and built up in him, strengthened in the faith as you were taught, and overflowing with thankfulness.

Philippians 2:5–11

⁵Your attitude should be the same as that of Christ Jesus:

> ⁶Who, being in very nature God,
>   did not consider equality with God
>   something to be grasped,
> ⁷but made himself nothing,
>   taking the very nature of a servant,
>   being made in human likeness.
> ⁸And being found in appearance as a man,
>   he humbled himself
>   and became obedient to death—
>   even death on a cross!
> ⁹Therefore God exalted him to the highest place
>   and gave him the name that is above every name,
> ¹⁰that at the name of Jesus every knee should bow,
>   in heaven and on earth and under the earth,
> ¹¹and every tongue confess that Jesus Christ
>   is Lord,
>   to the glory of God the Father.

Matthew 22:37–40

³⁷Jesus replied: " 'Love the Lord your God with all your heart and with all your soul and with all your mind.' ³⁸This is the first and greatest commandment. ³⁹And the second is like it: 'Love your neighbor as yourself.' ⁴⁰All the Law and the Prophets hang on these two commandments."

2 Corinthians 3:18

And we, who with unveiled faces all reflect the Lord's glory, are being transformed into his likeness with ever-increasing glory, which comes from the Lord, who is the Spirit.

1. According to Colossians 2, how should disciples of Jesus live their lives? What does it mean to become rooted and built up in Jesus?

_____

2. In Philippians 2, Paul talks about attitude, encouraging us as Christians to show the same attitude of humility that Jesus showed. Give some examples from Jesus' life that demonstrate how he "made himself nothing" and took "the very nature of a servant." Give some examples of how we can show that same attitude in our relationships.

_____

3. Philippians 2 also talks about Jesus' unfailing obedience. Give examples of ways in which we are to live obedient lives as Jesus did. (For a good place to start, reread Matthew 22:37–40.)

_____

4. According to 2 Corinthians 3:18, what happens to us when we live "in Christ"? Whose work is the work of sanctification—ours, God's, or a combination?

_____

5. Check the Scripture passages again. Can you find some characteristics of sanctified living you wish to add to the list you began earlier in the lesson? Now that you know what *sanctification* means, check your list to make sure each attribute you've listed really describes a follower of Christ.

_____

6. In your own words, write a personal definition of sanctification—a sentence or two that defines what is happening in your own life as you follow Jesus.

Discuss/Decide

Of all the areas in my life, one in which I need to become much more Christlike is . . .

To keep me from being like Jesus, Satan works hard to make me . . .

With the help of the Holy Spirit, I know I can become more . . .

Dear God,

Amen.

May the Mind of Christ, My Savior

1. May the mind of Christ, my Savior, live in me from day to day, by his love and power controlling all I do and say.
2. May the word of God dwell richly in my heart from hour to hour, so that all may see I triumph only through his power.
3. May the peace of God, my Father, rule my life in everything, that I may be calm to comfort sick and sorrowing.
4. May the love of Jesus fill me as the waters fill the sea. Him exalting, self abasing: this is victory.
5. May we run the race before us, strong and brave to face the foe, looking only unto Jesus as we onward go.

Text: Kate B. Wilkinson, 1925
Tune: A. Cyril Barham-Gould, 1925; desc. Emily R. Brink, 1986.
Tune by permission of the estate of A. C. Barham-Gould. Descant © 1987, CRC Publications

Lord, Make

Jerry stood hunched over outside the gym, his nose dripping blood onto the snow. Two friends consoled him, making sure he was OK and promising to help him get back at Paul. "You didn't do a thing—he just punched you. It's not right!" they said.

But Jerry didn't say a word. He was too mad to do a thing—too hurt, too embarrassed, too frustrated. How could this have happened?

The whole deal had built up over the last two weeks. Paul was a cocky kid; he didn't say much, but he had that look about him. Things got nasty when Paul wouldn't move to the top of the bleachers when Jerry and his friends ordered him to at the game last Tuesday. And when Jerry kicked him in the back to get him moving, Paul had spun around and called Jerry names. That led to more talk. Jerry reminded Paul he was just a dumb freshman who ought to keep his mouth shut. "Don't you have to leave now, kid? Aren't you supposed to be home by nine?" Jerry's taunts didn't quit.

After that night, Jerry's friends egged Paul on whenever they could. As they passed Paul and his freshman friends in the hall, they'd grin when Jerry bumped Paul with his shoulders, as if by accident. They'd laugh at Paul—a mean chuckle for his ears only. A chuckle that fed Paul's frustration.

But Paul's friends saw the pushes and heard the mean laughter. They urged Paul to shut Jerry up for good. "What he needs is a good fist in the mouth! Don't let him get to you, Paul!"

Then it happened. Another game, more push and shove in the bleachers, bad talk back and forth. "Come on outside at the half and we'll settle it, big guy!" grinned Jerry. "We'll see how tough you really are!" And at the half, Jerry's friends blocked Paul's

Us Forgiving

group in the narrow hallway outside the gym. There was no getting through.

That's when Paul threw his punch—straight at Jerry's nose. Jerry staggered back against the wall, giving Paul time to disappear with his crowd of friends. Jerry's crowd gave up the chase and helped their bloody friend out into the parking lot, where his nose sprayed the snow red.

The next week word raced through the corridors: Jerry was out to get Paul back! When Mr. D, the principal, heard about it, he set out to learn more. Jerry and Paul made separate trips to his office to tell Mr. D their separate stories. Separate stories that begged for a single ending.

Paul wanted a happy ending. He was ready to quit the unhappy business and apologize. He'd been mouthy and wrong. He shouldn't have hit Jerry, and he was ready to say so.

But Jerry wanted no part of it. "No way! Paul hit me, and I'm not going to drop it with a silly 'sorry'! Maybe it'll be this afternoon or maybe next month—but he'd better be ready. I'm not about to look like a wimp!"

So Mr. D called them in together. Jerry refused to look at Paul when Paul apologized for hitting him. "OK," Jerry mumbled. "But you ain't heard the end of this. If you weren't such a coward, you'd come out after school. We'll see who's tough." When Mr. D. talked about forgiveness and calling it quits, Jerry just growled, "Are you crazy? Of course I won't. I can't. My honor's on the line. I'm a man—NOT a wimp!"

Paul just shrugged his shoulders and said he had to leave. He promised not to start a fight—but he promised not to run away from one either. Jerry left too. He smiled a crazy smile, a determined smile. He'd get even . . .

LESSON 7

The Parable of the Un

Peter came to Jesus and asked, "Lord, how many times shall I forgive my brother when he sins against me? Up to seven times?"

Jesus answered, "I tell you, not seven times, but seventy-seven times."

To emphasize his point, Jesus told a story that sounded something like this short drama:

CAST OF CHARACTERS

Mr. T: A very rich man who owns much land and employs many people to care for his property

Joe: A hired man who has borrowed money from Mr. T and can't meet the payment deadline

Sam: A friend who owes Joe money

Situation: *Mr. T has decided he wants to settle up all old accounts and call in all loans he has made. One person who still owes him money is his hired man, Joe.*

Mr. T: Hey Joe, remember that $90,000 I lent you three years ago? Your payment date is way past due, but I haven't mentioned it. Can you pay it back to me by next Wednesday?

Joe: (*nervous; fumbling for words*) I'm sorry, sir, I just don't have the money yet. Times have been rough. I thought I'd have made it up by now, but that investment I made with your loan just didn't work out. Please . . . can I have a little more time? Something should come through in the next six months or so.

Mr. T: Sorry, Joe, a deal's a deal. You knew about the arrangements when I gave you the money. I'm afraid I'll have to foreclose on your property. You'll probably have to sell your land and your truck. I need the money by Wednesday . . . at the latest!

Joe: (*on his knees, tearful, begging*) Sir! Please don't do that! Just give me a little more time—two weeks maybe. I'll repay everything, I promise. I will!

Mr. T: (*shaking his head with a sigh and pausing to think about it*) Well . . . OK. I can see what a fix you're in. Just forget the loan altogether. I can handle it.

Merciful Servant

Several hours later Joe storms into the hardware store where he finds his friend, Sam, working in the back room.

Joe: (*grabs Sam by the neck, shaking him and screaming at him*) OK buddy, pay up! I know you've got my ten bucks! You've been holding out on me! Hand it over—now!

Sam: (*stumbling backward against the wall, escaping Joe's choke hold*) Hey, Joe, take it easy! I know I owe you. I promised I'd pay it back, didn't I? All I need is a little more time . . . give me two days, OK?

Joe: No way, man! I'm sick of it! Pay me now or I'll take you to court. Count on it!

When word of the incident between Joe and Sam got around, Mr. T called Joe into his office.

Mr. T: Joe, I hear you've been threatening Sam over a few dollars he owes you. How could you? Here I cancel your debt because I feel so sorry for you; then you turn around and treat your buddy like he's a common criminal! Have you no heart, man? Forget your land and truck . . . they're mine now. And I want the rest of what you owe me by tomorrow—or it's prison.

Then Jesus ended his story with these words: "This is how my heavenly Father will treat each of you unless you forgive your brother from your heart."

(based on Matthew 18:21–35)

Discuss/Decide

1. Jesus answers Peter's question in Matthew 18:21 by telling him to forgive someone seventy-seven times. What is the point of Jesus' answer?

2. The little story Jesus told is a parable, a story with a central meaning that helps us see our proper relationship to God and his people. What is the central meaning of this parable?

3. In the drama based on Jesus' parable, what is the point of the big difference between the amounts owed in the two debts?

4. In Matthew 18:35, Jesus asks us to forgive people "from the heart." What does he mean?

5. Recall the words of the Lord's Prayer as you studied it a few weeks ago (lesson 4). Which request from that prayer does this parable illustrate?

What Would You Do If . . .

—your mother said you could go to a roller-skating party but at the last minute said she needed you to stay home and baby-sit?

—you had been iced out of a group of girlfriends for five weeks and Lisa, one of the girls in the group, meets you at your locker and asks you to be her friend again?

—your dad walked out on your family, was out of touch for three months, and came back wanting to resume a normal family life?

—your math teacher accused you (in front of the whole class) of cheating on a test? You're innocent and feel unfairly accused (and very embarrassed!).

—your brother "borrowed" your best shirt (without asking, of course) and returned it, stained and wrinkled, without comment?

Q. What does the fifth request mean?

A. *Forgive us our debts,
as we also have forgiven our debtors*
means,

Because of Christ's blood,
do not hold against us, poor sinners that
we are,
any of the sins we do
or the evil that constantly clings to us.

Forgive us just as we are fully determined,
as evidence of your grace in us,
to forgive our neighbors.

Heidelberg Catechism Q & A 126

When Abraham Lincoln was President of the United States, he received a visit at the White House from a woman pleading with the guards to see him. She had come on behalf of her son, a soldier who had been sentenced to death for falling asleep at 4:00 A.M. while on guard duty. Finally, well past midnight, Lincoln allowed the guards to let her in to speak with him. She tearfully explained that her son, conscripted to fight in the Civil War for the Union, was only fourteen years old. After listening to the mother, Lincoln is said to have responded something like this: "I know how much I liked to sleep when I was a lad that age—one can't expect more from him. I pardon him of the charge."

(Based on *Abraham Lincoln: The War Years, Vol. III*,
New York: Harcourt, Brace & Company, 1939, pp. 528–529.)

As a Red Cross nurse in Belgium during World War I, Edith Cavell helped Allied soldiers escape from behind enemy lines. The Germans captured her and sentenced her to death. As Edith was led before the firing squad, she is reputed to have said, "I realize that patriotism is not enough; I must have no hatred or bitterness toward anyone."

(Taken from the *Oxford Dictionary of Quotations* as printed in
The Little, Brown Book of Anecdotes, ed. by Clifton Fadiman,
copyright 1985, Little, Brown and Company, Inc.)

One day in 1981 Pope John Paul II, one of the truly great popes of the twentieth century, was greeting people from his open car in St. Peter's Square in Rome. Suddenly he catapulted backward, collapsing into the arms of his security people. The Pope had been shot by a would-be assassin, Mehmet Ali Agca. The scene ended as the Popemobile moved away, helpers shielding the stricken John Paul.

Almost three years later there was another scene which most of the world saw and will never forget. It was a scene of grace. Pope John Paul II entered the prison cell where Mehmet Ali Agca was serving his life sentence. The two men talked. The Pope grasped Agca's arm. Speaking softly, John Paul forgave Agca for trying to kill him. Agca, a Muslim who was not familiar with Christian forgiveness, seemed confused. But at the end of the meeting Agca pressed the Pope's hand to his face, as if to express respect.

(Taken from *A Sure Thing* by Cornelius Plantinga, Jr. Copyright © 1986, CRC Publications, p. 150.)

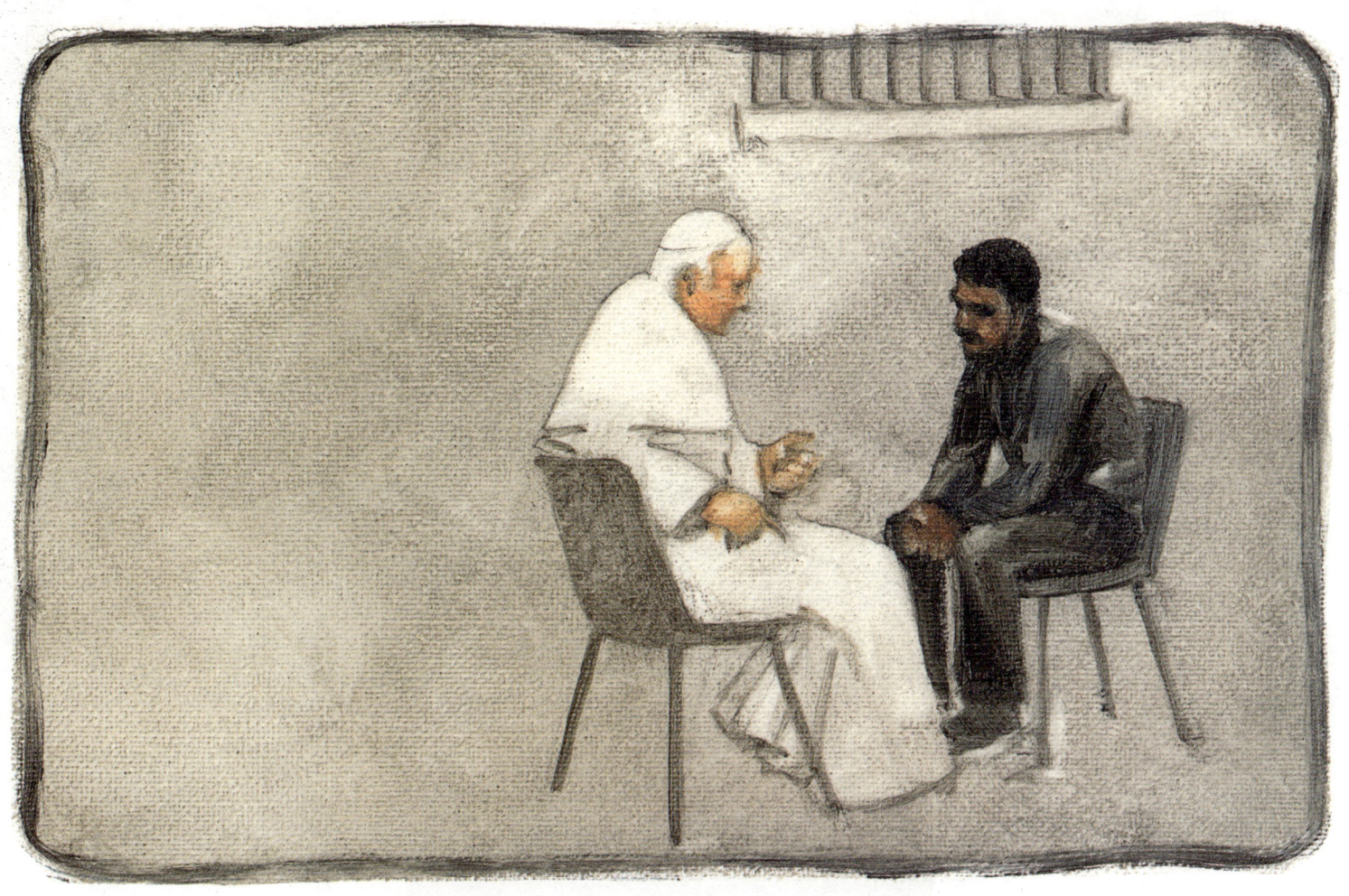

Lord, Discipline Our

LESSON 8

Lives

Self-discipline is . . .

One area in my life in which I need self-discipline is . . .

One way I work at disciplining myself is . . .

The Big Race

I couldn't believe it. I had qualified for the finals of the state track meet, and this was the big day.

Ever since I was 8 years old, I'd watched the summer Olympics and the NCAA championship meets, and if there was anything I wanted, it was to run in one of those events. I made up my mind that I was going to, and winning the state high-school meet had to be the first step. Four months before this meet, I had given up everything, even basketball, just to start running. I had to get in shape. Last year, when I was a sophomore, I loafed through spring practice and finished the half-mile in fifth place. My coaches were satisfied, my friends were satisfied—everybody was satisfied except me, because I knew I could have done better with more work.

This year the coach, Mr. Cooper, and the assistant coach, Mr. Brookhart, were new, and they cared—boy, they really cared. The first day of official practice I came home sicker than a dog and I went straight to bed, despising track and everything it stood for. But when the first couple of meets came rolling by and I finished with two firsts and a second, I began to enjoy it. I went ripping into April with the sixth fastest half-mile and the tenth best quarter-mile in the state. Then came the big meets with all of the metropolitan schools. Here is where the work really counted. In the Denver Metro Meet with 18 schools, I finished second in the half-mile.

I seemed to do better as the competition increased. The preliminaries in the state track meet were held the night before the finals, and I had the second fastest time. I seemed a sure bet to place in the finals.

Now here I was. They were calling first call for the 800-meter run over the loudspeaker. My heart seemed to jump and then stop somewhere in my throat. It felt like a boxing match was going on in my stomach. I could hardly breathe. I ran up and down beside the track a few times to see if I could loosen up—loosen up! I was getting more tense all of the time.

I wanted to pray that I would win, but that would mean that I was praying for someone else to lose, and I couldn't do that. Every guy there wanted to win as much as I did.

Last call for the 800-meter run. As I reported, they called our names over the speaker. I had a bad place, on the outside lane.

The starter said, "On your mark . . . Get ready . . ." The gun was up, and I jumped it. A false start. If I did it again, I would be disqualified.

The gun went off. Because I was on the outside, I was out in front. It's hard to know, when you're in this position, just how fast to go. If you start out too fast, you don't have anything left at the finish.

Those on the inside lanes were moving up on me. I let them pass, I always run near the middle until the last lap, and then I pour it on. I was still somewhere in the middle as we finished the first lap. As we rounded the third turn, I moved to the outside to pass, and just as I did, someone caught my left foot. I began to stumble—two, three steps, and then I was lying on the track.

It seemed I was there a long time, but in reality it must only have been a moment, while I decided whether to finish the race or walk off the track. I didn't stand a chance now of coming in anywhere, but I wasn't a quitter, so I decided to finish.

The coach was waiting for me. He didn't say anything; he just put his arm around my shoulders. My elbow and knee were cut and smarting, but those cuts didn't go as deep as my disappointment.

In 17 years of life this was the worst thing that had ever happened to me. I had always believed that what often seemed a calamity would later turn out to be best. It was hard to look at this in the same way, especially that evening; but the more I thought about it, the more I thought, *My faith has always worked for me before, why not now?*

I opened my Bible, and God must have been guiding me, for I turned right to Psalm 37. My eye fell on verse 24, and he was speaking to me:

"Though he stumble, he will not fall, for the Lord upholds him with his hand."

I felt better. It is easy to have faith when things are going right, but now I knew that God was there even when things didn't go right.

Now a year has passed, and since I am a senior, this is the most important year. I do not know how this year's meet will go, but I know that because of my disappointment last year, I am working even harder to achieve what I missed then. Maybe that was God's plan.

("The Big Race" by John Morton, reprinted with permission from *Guideposts Magazine*. Copyright © 1972 by Guideposts Associates, Inc. Carmel, New York 10512.)

Philippians 3:12–14 (TEV)

¹²I do not claim that I have already succeeded or have already become perfect. I keep striving to win the prize for which Christ Jesus has already won me to himself. ¹³Of course, my brothers, I really do not think that I have already won it; the one thing I do, however, is to forget what is behind me and do my best to reach what is ahead. ¹⁴So I run straight toward the goal in order to win the prize, which is God's call through Christ Jesus to the life above.

1 Corinthians 9:24–25

²⁴Do you not know that in a race all the runners run, but only one gets the prize? Run in such a way as to get the prize. ²⁵Everyone who competes in the games goes into strict training. They do it to get a crown that will not last; but we do it to get a crown that will last forever.

James 1:12

Blessed is the man who perseveres under trial, because when he has stood the test, he will receive the crown of life [victor's wreath] that God has promised to those who love him.

Discuss/Decide

1. What pictures come to your mind when you read these passages describing the self-disciplined life of Christ's disciples? Underline words or phrases that suggest that disciples of Christ are a lot like athletes.

2. To train with discipline, athletes usually set goals for themselves. What kinds of goals do you set for yourself as an athlete, as a student, as a musician, and so on? Describe the goal that kept Paul on track as a disciple of Jesus.

3. To achieve their goals, athletes have to discover their weak areas and work hard to perfect or improve themselves. In what areas of your life do you take time to identify weaknesses and work to correct them? What does Paul have to say about overcoming weakness and striving for perfection as disciples of Jesus?

4. For an athlete, keeping an eye on the goal often means giving up things that would be distracting and would stand in the way of an excellent performance. Setting priorities—and sticking to them—also requires self-discipline. Read the story of the rich young ruler (below) who wished to follow Jesus; then answer the following questions:
   a. What did the rich young ruler see as his strengths? Did Jesus agree?
   b. What did Jesus point out as the rich young ruler's weakness, the roadblock that might prevent him from becoming a disciple of Christ?
   c. How did the rich young ruler show he lacked the self-discipline it takes to be Christ's disciple?
   d. What did Jesus (v. 21) mean by his answer to the rich young man's question?

5. What comfort do you find in Matthew 19? Circle any words or phrases that encourage you as a disciple of Jesus.

Matthew 19:16–26

¹⁶Now a man came up to Jesus and asked, "Teacher, what good thing must I do to get eternal life?"

¹⁷"Why do you ask me about what is good?" Jesus replied. "There is only One who is good. If you want to enter life, obey the commandments."

¹⁸"Which ones?" the man inquired.

Jesus replied, " 'Do not murder, do not commit adultery, do not steal, do not give false testimony, ¹⁹honor your father and mother,' and 'love your neighbor as yourself.' "

²⁰"All these I have kept," the young man said. "What do I still lack?"

²¹Jesus answered, "If you want to be perfect, go sell your possessions and give to the poor, and you will have treasure in heaven. Then come, follow me."

²²When the young man heard this, he went away sad, because he had great wealth.

²³Then Jesus said to his disciples, "I tell you the truth, it is hard for a rich man to enter the kingdom of heaven. ²⁴Again I tell you, it is easier for a camel to go through the eye of a needle than for a rich man to enter the kingdom of God."

²⁵When the disciples heard this, they were greatly astonished and asked, "Who then can be saved?"

²⁶Jesus looked at them and said, "With man this is impossible, but with God all things are possible."

HURDLES!

Knowing what you do about yourself and other Christians around you, which of the following hurdles seems to be the hardest to overcome for a person who seeks to follow Jesus? Put a *1* in front of the hurdle that seems to be the highest hurdle, a *2* in front of the second, and so forth. When you've finished, compare notes with each other to see how the class ranked each one. Why do some hurdles seem so high and so hard to jump over?

____ insecurity (I'm not important!)

____ pride (I'm the best!)

____ materialism (I love my possessions!)

____ friends (My friends come first in my life.)

____ fun (I want to party!)

____ laziness (Don't push me too hard!)

____ looks (Clothes are important to me.)

____ sports (All I want to do is play ball.)

____ music (Who needs anything else?)

____ other

____ other

Dear Lord,

The hurdle that sometimes keeps me from following Jesus is . . .

Please give me self-discipline so I can . . .

Help me to keep my eyes on this goal as I follow Jesus . . .

Amen.

Lord, Give Us Courage

LESSON 9

Try to picture what it means to be a follower of Jesus. Some people might visualize a light shining in the darkness, a sign of God's people being lights in a dark world. Others might see a shepherd (Jesus) caring for his flock (us). Still others might picture willing hands bringing a cup of cold water to a thirsty person. Someone might imagine a field of brightly colored flowers or balloons dancing across a deep-blue sky, both signs of celebration and joy.

Use your imagination to think of a picture or symbol that says something to *you* about what it's like to be Jesus' disciple. Sketch or describe your idea in box at right:

"If anyone would come after me, he must deny himself and take up his cross and follow me."

—Jesus (Matthew 16:24)

How did the apostles "take up their crosses" after Jesus ascended into heaven? The Bible gives us few details about the apostles' suffering and death, but stories and symbols handed down by Christians from generation to generation desribe what *might* have happened to some of the twelve disciples and the apostle Paul.

Match the names of the apostles to the descriptions and symbols below. The Scripture references will tell you the answers.

APOSTLES

Andrew

Bartholomew (Nathanael)

James, son of Alphaeus

James, son of Zebedee

John

Paul

Peter

Thomas

Simon the Zealot

1. _____
This apostle once "boasted" that because he followed Jesus he had been beaten eight times, stoned once, and shipwrecked three times (2 Cor. 11:22–25). His symbol is an open Bible and sword. The Latin words written on the Bible mean *sword of the Spirit,* a term he used to describe God's Word (Eph. 6:17).

2. _____
This apostle was one of the "Sons of Thunder" (Mark 3:17). Jesus said that this disciple would have to drink the cup his Master was to drink. These words came true when this apostle became the first of the apostles to die as a martyr, beheaded by King Agrippa about ten years after Jesus' ascension (Acts 12:2). The sword in his symbol stands for his beheading. The scallop shell represents his missionary journeys, which may have taken him to Spain.

3. _____
With his brother Peter, this apostle was a fisherman by trade (Matt. 4:18). Tradition says that he was crucified in Greece on an X-shaped cross (see his symbol). To prolong his suffering, he was tied, rather than nailed, to the cross.

4. _____
Tradition says that after Christ's ascension, this apostle traveled to East India where he built a church with his own hands (see the carpenter's square in his symbol). The stories also say that he died a cruel death. He was first shot with arrows and then speared by a pagan priest (see spear on his symbol). This apostle is best known for what he doubted (John 20:25).

7. _____
"I will give you the keys of the kingdom of heaven," Jesus told this apostle (Matt. 16:19). Jesus also said that this apostle would die a martyr's death (John 21:18–19). According to tradition, he was crucified upside down (see symbol), considering himself unworthy to be crucified in the same position as his Lord.

5. _____
Little is known about this disciple, whose name is mentioned in Matthew 10:3, Mark 15:40, and Acts 1:13. Sometimes "the younger" is added to his name. Tradition says that he was pushed off the pinnacle of the temple and stoned to death. His symbol is a saw because, according to tradition, his body was sawed into pieces.

8. _____
Little is known about this disciple, whose name suggests he may have been very diligent in opposing Roman rule in Palestine (see last name mentioned in Mark 3:18). It is very likely that he became head of the Jerusalem church. He may have made missionary journeys to Africa or Persia. The fish in his symbol is a mark of his missionary success, and the book is a symbol of the gospel. Tradition says he was either beheaded or sawed to death.

6. _____
This apostle could be the same man mentioned in John 1:47. Although the Bible tells us little about him, the stories say that he converted the king of Armenia to Christianity. The king's brother was so angered by the conversion that he had this apostle flayed with knives (see symbol) and crucified.

9. _____
The eagle, which flies at great heights, is the symbol for this apostle, whose inspired writings (five New Testament books) lifted his readers to great spiritual heights. "Because of the word of God and the testimony of Jesus" he was exiled to the small rocky island of Patmos (Rev. 1:9).

(Symbols and facts reprinted with permission from *Symbol Cards* packet of 54 cards, published by the National Teacher Education Program, 2504 N. Roxboro St., Durham, NC 27704.)

Bearing Our Crosses

No one wants to carry a cross. Even Jesus pleaded with his Father to spare him from the suffering of the cross. Fortunately, Christians don't need to carry crosses to earn their salvation; Jesus did that once and for all on Calvary.

Even so, all of Jesus' disciples face trials and troubles that test their faith and their commitment to their Lord. These trials and troubles are our "crosses" to carry. Although some of our suffering comes because we're Christians, much of it comes because we live in a sinful world.

Do you know a Christian who has suffered a great deal? If so, take time to think about that person and how he or she has reacted to his or her "cross."

Read through the list of trials and troubles (below) that have already come or could come into your life. (If you wish, add to the list in the space provided.) When you're finished, mark an "X" by those trials that you have experienced or will likely experience because you follow Jesus.

"I can do everything through him who gives me strength."
—Paul
(Phil. 4:13)

_____ getting sick or injured

_____ fighting between parents; divorce

_____ being snubbed by your friends after helping somebody whom others mock

_____ being thought of as super righteous after refusing to do something wrong

_____ being financially poor in comparison to those around you

_____ doing poorly in school

_____ experiencing the death of someone very close to you

_____ being the victim of racial slurs

_____ having a really stupid nickname

_____ being unable to do things non-Christians can do

_____ being too fat or skinny

_____ being lonely

_____ other: _____

When trials and troubles come our way, where do we get the courage to face that suffering (see Phil. 4:11–13)?

What can we learn about how to face suffering from Jesus' struggle in the Garden of Gethsemane (see Matt. 26:36–39)?

Can we ever *benefit* from suffering? Explain.

Footprints

One night a man had a dream. He dreamed he was walking along the beach with the Lord. Across the sky flashed scenes from his life. For each scene, he noticed two sets of footprints in the sand; one belonging to him, and the other to the Lord.

When the last scene of his life flashed before him, he looked back at the footprints in the sand. He noticed that many times along the path of his life there was only one set of footprints. He also noticed that it happened at the very lowest and saddest times in his life.

This really bothered him, and he questioned the Lord about it. "Lord, you said that once I decided to follow you, you'd walk with me all the way. But I have noticed that during the most troublesome times in my life there is only one set of footprints. I don't understand why when I needed you the most you would leave me."

The Lord replied, "My child, my precious child, I love you and I would never leave you. During your times of trial and suffering, when you see only one set of footprints, it was then that I carried you."

Author Unknown

Q. What is your only comfort in life and in death?

A. That I am not my own,
   but belong—
      body and soul,
      in life and in death—
to my faithful Savior Jesus Christ.

    He has fully paid for all my sins with his precious blood,
    and has set me free from the tyranny of the devil.
    He also watches over me in such a way
    that not a hair can fall from my head
    without the will of my Father in heaven:
    in fact, all things must work together for my salvation.

Because I belong to him,
Christ, by his Holy Spirit,
assures me of eternal life
and makes me wholeheartedly willing and ready
from now on to live for him.

Heidelberg Catechism Q & A 1

Psalm 89

I feel like singing this morning, O Lord.
I feel like telling everyone around me
    how great You are.
If only they could know the depths of Your love
    and Your eternal concern for those
        who will follow You!
But my songs are so often off-key.
My speech is so inadequate.
I simply cannot express what I feel,
    what I know to be true about Your love
        for Your creatures upon this world.

But even the songs of the birds
    proclaim Your praises.
The heavens and the earth beneath them,
    the trees that reach toward You,
    the flowers that glow in colorful beauty,
    the green hills and soaring mountains,
    the valleys and the plains,
    the lakes and the rivers,
    the great oceans that pound our shores—
    they proclaim Your greatness, O God,
    and Your love for the sons of men.

How glorious it is to be alive, O Lord!
May every breath of my body,
    every beat of my heart,
        be dedicated to Your praise and glory.

by Leslie F. Brandt

(Reprinted from *Psalms/Now*, copyright © 1973, Concordia Publishing House. Reprinted by permission from CPH.)

I feel like singing this morning, O Lord.
I feel like telling everyone around me
    how great You are . . .
For all these things I give you thanks . . .

How glorious it is to be alive, O Lord!
May every breath of my body,
    every beat of my heart,
        be dedicated to Your praise and glory.

LESSON 10

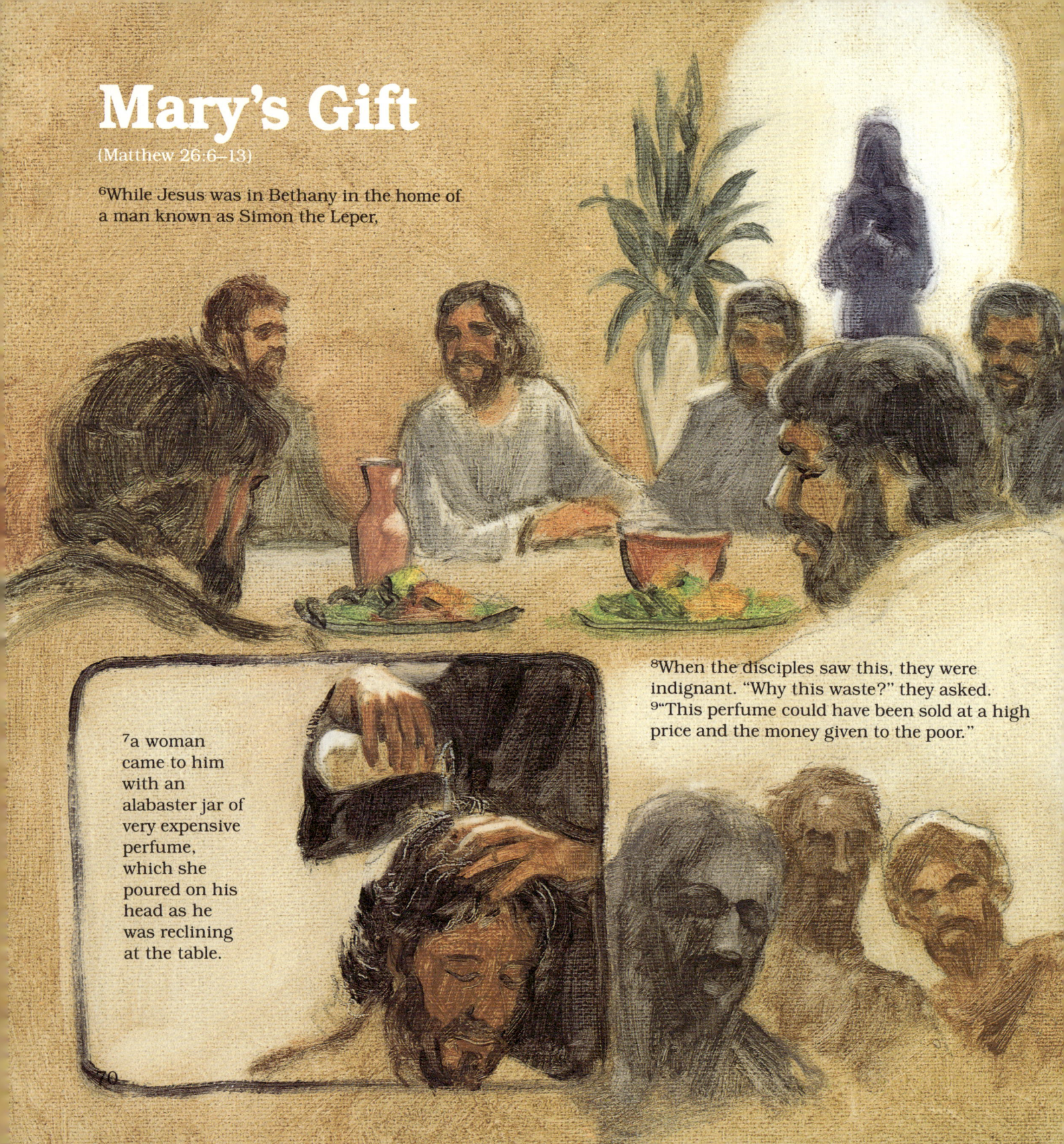

Mary's Gift
(Matthew 26:6–13)

⁶While Jesus was in Bethany in the home of a man known as Simon the Leper,

⁷a woman came to him with an alabaster jar of very expensive perfume, which she poured on his head as he was reclining at the table.

⁸When the disciples saw this, they were indignant. "Why this waste?" they asked. ⁹"This perfume could have been sold at a high price and the money given to the poor."

Discuss/Decide

1. Imagine yourself as Mary. You've sat at Jesus' feet, listened to him, and learned from him. You are his friend and follower. What one word sums up the feelings that led to the purchase of such an expensive gift for your Master? How did you feel when you presented your gift to Jesus?

2. Imagine yourself as a dinner guest observing Mary's act of thankfulness. What is your reaction? What are the disciples around you saying about the act?

3. What was Jesus' reaction to the disciples' criticism of Mary's gift? Why didn't Jesus compliment them on their concern for the poor? Why did he compliment Mary instead, calling her act a "beautiful thing"?

4. What does Scripture suggest Mary's gift intended to accomplish in addition to showing her thanks (see v. 13)?

5. Suggest some ways in which we can offer actions of thanks to Jesus. Do thankful acts please Jesus more than thankful words? How costly (in terms of time, money, talent, etc.) do our acts of thanks need to be in order to be "beautiful" gifts?

Write Your Own Meditation . . .

Scripture is bursting with exclamations of praise and thanks to the Lord from his people. Here are a few references that are either a call to give thanks or actual expressions of thanks from God's children: Psalm 9:1–2; Psalm 33:1–4; Psalm 100; Psalm 136:1–4; Luke 1:46–55; Luke 17:11–19; Colossians 2:6–7; Colossians 3:15–17. Look up one of the passages and think about it for a few minutes. Then write down your thoughts as you put together a short meditation on the verses. Here's a model to follow:

SCRIPTURE:

THOUGHTS ABOUT IT:

ASK YOURSELF:

PRAYER:

Abundant Thanks!

One day in late December I went to the slums of Kivulu to collect an orphaned child, one of two children in Kivulu that I had once walked to Sunday School. *Kivulu*, "the mixture," was located just below the university on the lower slopes of Makerere Hill. Its streets were narrow and crowded, and I left my car on the nearest main road. . . .

It was teatime when I arrived at the child's home. Her guardian, Miriyamu, greeted me at the door and showed me to a wooden bench in the outer room. The dirt floor had been swept clean and the whole room tidied. In the corner was a charcoal stove and a short wooden shelf holding a few cups and plates. They were smoked and stained from age, but not dirty.

"Please wait here," Miriyamu said to me politely. "I will bring the child, Topista."

She stepped into the back room and a few minutes later returned with a small child of six or seven. Topista was dressed in her best garment, and her face had been freshly oiled—possibly a bit too much—with Vaseline. She knelt down and greeted me shyly.

At just that moment the teakettle boiled. Miriyamu exclaimed and hurried to remove it from the flame. With a polite apology she excused herself and stepped again to the back room. After a few minutes of noisy rattling she returned. In her hands was a brand-new porcelain cup.

In the darkness of the front room, the porcelain cup gleamed. It gleamed on the mud wall, on the dirt floor, on the soiled garments of Miriyamu and Topista. There was nothing in the room that it did not outshine. Miriyamu wiped it carefully and placed it gently on an old rusty tray. She took other cups from the shelf and filled them all with tea. Then, with deep pleasure and goodwill, Miriyamu gave the porcelain cup to me.

It was a special favor I had received many times before. It was the special favor the very poor reserved for the *abaana babowo*, the privileged class. I took the cup and sat down on the bench to drink my tea. Miriyamu rolled out a mat and sat on the floor with Topista. For a few minutes we spoke together about coffee and cotton prediction, and the tribal conflict in the north. When I finished my tea, I stood up from the bench and returned the cup to Miriyamu. She placed it gently back on the tray. She nodded to Topista and Topista too rose to leave. But first, as every good child does, she knelt before her guardian and said good-bye. Miriyamu's eyes shone with joy, "This is a most happy day," she said. "This is the day your life begins again."

As we walked out the door, I remembered the bedding. To help the children in the period of transition, it was our policy at the home to have them bring their own mats and blankets. I spoke to Miriyamu, but she shook her head. Topista had no mat. She had only a torn and soiled blanket. It was a blanket she placed on the dirt floor in the evening and blanket she carefully folded up again in the morning. But it was not, Miriyamu said in humble apology, a blanket with which to start a new life.

Topista and I drove to the children's home, and on our way we

ughed and joked. But in my mind I
as saying, *This frivolous Miriyamu,
is woman of no understanding.
hy does she have a porcelain cup
hen Topista has no mat?* And then
hought, *No wonder the poor are
or. No wonder strangers come and
llect their children.*

That evening I told Penina the
hole story of Miriyamu and the
orcelain cup. It was only my own
gry thought that I kept to myself.

"Isn't that something!" Penina
id when I finished my story. She
iled with pleasure. "The poor have
ch deep understanding!"

These were not the words I had
pected to hear. *Perhaps,* I thought
myself *Penina has not understood.
e has not understood that the
ild Topista has no bed.*

But Penina was still speaking.
he humble poor," she said, "know
deep secret. They give from
emselves, not from their surplus.
ey give from the abundance of
eir hearts."

(aken from *A Distant Grief* by F. Kefa Sempangi.
opyright © 1980, Regal Books, Ventura, CA 93006.
sed by permission.)

THINK ABOUT IT . . .

1. Does Miriyamu's expression of thanks for Topista's new life remind you of Mary's story in today's Scripture lesson? How is the writer of the story a bit like Jesus' disciples?

2. What do both stories suggest about how we should praise and thank Jesus for the new life he gives us?

Father, We Love You

1 Fa- ther,
2 Je- sus, we love you, we wor- ship, we a- dore you,
3 Spir- it,

glo- ri- fy your name in all the earth,
glo- ri- fy your name, glo- ri- fy your name,
glo- ri- fy your name in all the earth.

Text and Tune: Donna Adkins, 1976; harm. Dale Grotenhuis, 1985. © 1976, 1981, Maranatha! Music c/o The Copyright Company, Nashville, TN. All rights reserved. International copyright secured. Used by permission.

Lord, Help Us Grow

Who's Growing?

For the following list of actions, make a judgment about the *percentage* of young people you know that the statement describes. For example, you might think that 90% love Jesus but hide it. Or you may think it's more like 50% or 10%.

When you're finished, compare your guesses with your classmates.

WHAT PERCENTAGE OF YOUNG PEOPLE YOU KNOW . . .

_____ 1. just ignore God?

_____ 2. love Jesus but hide it most of the time?

_____ 3. think their faith is stronger than that of other kids?

_____ 4. experience ups and downs in their spiritual lives?

_____ 5. are growing as Christians?

_____ 6. seem to be better Christians than you are?

LESSON 11

The Rock that Grew

CAST
Narrator 1
Narrator 2
Jesus
Disciples
Peter
Servant Girl 1
Servant Girl 2
People in Crowd

SCENE 1
A Big Decision
(based on Matthew 4:18–20)

Narrator 1
  As Jesus was walking beside the Sea of Galilee, he saw two brothers, Simon called Peter and his brother Andrew. They were casting a net into the lake, for they were fishermen.
Jesus
  Come, follow me, and I will make you fishers of men.
Narrator 2
  At once they left their nets and followed him.

> **Discuss/Decide**
> 1. What does this scene tell us about Peter?

SCENE 2
Peter's Big Scene
(based on Matthew 16:13–19)

Narrator 1
  When Jesus came to the region of Caesarea Philippi, he asked his disciples an important question.
Jesus
  Who do people say the Son of Man is?
Disciples
  Some say John the Baptist; others say Elijah; and still others, Jeremiah or one or the prophets.
Jesus
  But what about you? Who do you say that I am?
Peter
  You are the Christ, the Son of the living God.
Jesus
  Blessed are you, Simon, son of Jonah, for this was not revealed to you by man, but by my Father in heaven. And I tell you that you are Peter, and on this rock I will build my church, and the gates of Hades

will not overcome it. I will give you the keys of the kingdom of heaven; whatever you bind on earth will be bound in heaven, and whatever you loose on earth will be loosed in heaven.

> **Discuss/Decide**
>
> 2. This is Peter's big scene. Why?
>
> 3. What does it take to confess Jesus as Peter did?

SCENE 3
A Big Promise
(based on Matthew 26:31–35)

Narrator 2
Jesus and his disciples had just celebrated the Passover meal together. After singing a hymn, they went out to the Mount of Olives.

Jesus
This very night you will all fall away on account of me.

Peter
Even if all fall away on account of you, I never will.

Jesus
I tell you the truth, this very night, before the rooster crows, you will disown me three times.

Peter
Even if I have to die with you, I will never disown you.

Narrator 1
And all the other disciples said the same.

> **Discuss/Decide**
>
> 4. Say Peter's promise the way you think he said it. Why would he say such a thing?
>
> 5. When might we think that our faith is stronger than it actually is?

SCENE 4
A Big Disappointment
(based on Matthew 26:69–75)

Narrator 2
Now Peter was sitting out in the courtyard, and a servant girl came to him.

Servant Girl 1
You also were with Jesus of Galilee.

Peter
I don't know what you're talking about.

Narrator 1
Then he went out to the gateway, where another girl saw him and said to the people there . . .

Servant Girl 2
This fellow was with Jesus of Nazareth.

Peter
I don't know the man!

People in Crowd
Surely you are one of them, for your accent gives you away.

Narrator 2
Then Peter began to call down curses on himself, and he swore he didn't know Jesus.

Peter
I don't know the man!

Narrator 1

Immediately a rooster crowed. Then Peter remembered the words Jesus had spoken: "Before the rooster crows, you will disown me three times." And he went outside and wept bitterly.

Discuss/Decide

6. Why do you think Peter denied knowing Jesus?

7. Why did he "weep bitterly"?

8. In what ways do we sometimes say to others, "I'm not a follower of Jesus"?

SCENE 5
Three Very Big Questions
(based on John 21:7–19)

Narrator 2

For the third time, Jesus appeared to his disciples after he was raised from the dead. The disciples had been fishing all night. When they landed, they saw a fire of burning coals with fish on it, and some bread.

Jesus

Bring some of the fish you have just caught.

Narrator 1

Simon Peter dragged the net ashore. It was full of large fish, but even with so many the net was not torn.

Jesus

Come and have breakfast.

Narrator 2

When they had finished eating, Jesus began talking with Simon Peter.

Jesus

Simon son of John, do you truly love me more than these?

Peter

Yes, Lord, you know that I love you.

Jesus

Feed my lambs. Simon son of John, do you truly love me?

Peter

Yes, Lord, you know that I love you.

Jesus

Take care of my sheep. Simon son of John, do you love me?

Narrator 1

Peter was hurt because Jesus asked him the third time, "Do you love me?" But he answered anyway . . .

Peter

Lord, you know all things; you know that I love you.

Jesus

Feed my sheep. I tell you the truth, when you were younger you dressed yourself and went where you wanted; but when you are old you will stretch out your hands, and someone else will dress you and lead you where you do not want to go.

Narrator 2
Jesus said this to indicate the kind of death by which Peter would glorify God. Then Jesus said to Peter . . .
Jesus
Follow me.

> Discuss/Decide
> 9. Why did Jesus ask Peter the same question three times? How do you think Peter felt after this talk with Jesus? What comforts you in this scene?

SCENE 6
A Little Advice
(based on 1 Peter 5:8–11)

Narrator 1
Years later, Peter wrote a letter to the Christians scattered throughout Asia Minor. His advice was that of an older and wiser apostle, someone whose faith had grown tremendously.
Peter
Be self-controlled and alert. Your enemy the devil prowls around like a roaring lion looking for someone to devour. Resist him, standing firm in the faith, because you know that your brothers throughout the world are undergoing the same kind of sufferings.

And the God of all grace, who called you to his eternal glory in Christ, after you have suffered a little while, will himself restore you and make you strong, firm and steadfast. To him be the power for ever and ever. Amen.

> Discuss/Decide
> 10. What do you think Peter learned from his experience? Look at his letter (above) for clues.
>
> 11. How could the following people grow from their mistakes?
> A. Ryan was telling a juicy and untrue story about Jeff, when suddenly he realized that Jeff was standing behind him, listening to every word.
> B. Amy cheated regularly in Mr. Moore's math class. She felt she wasn't doing anything wrong because lots of the kids cheated, and Mr. Moore never noticed. Besides, math was her worse subject. She hated it. One day, as she leaned to one side to copy Lynn's answer, she felt Mr. Moore's hand on her shoulder. She was caught.
>
> If you can, give your own example of someone who grew closer to God through a painful failure.

A Very Bad Man

Once a very bad man died and went before the judgment throne. Before him stood Abraham, David, Peter, and Luke. A chilly silence hung heavy in the room as an unseen voice began to read the details of the man's life. There was nothing good that was recorded. When the voice concluded, Abraham spoke: "Men like you cannot enter the heavenly kingdom. You must leave."

"Father Abraham," the man cried, "I do not defend myself. I have no choice but to ask for mercy. Certainly you understand. Though you lied to save your own life, saying your wife was your sister, by the grace and mercy of God you became a blessing to all nations."

David interrupted, "Abraham has spoken correctly. You have committed evil and heinous crimes. You do not belong in the kingdom of light."

The man faced the great king and cried, "Son of Jesse, it is true. I am a wicked man. Yet I dare ask you for forgiveness. You slept with Uriah's wife and later, to cover your sin, arranged his death. I ask only forgiveness as you have known it."

Peter was next to speak. "Unlike David, you have shown no love to God. By your acid tongue and vile temper you have wounded the Son of God."

"I should be silent," the man muttered. "The only way I have used the blessed name of Jesus is in anger. Still, Simon, son of John, I plead for grace. Though you walked by his side and listened to words from his own lips, you slept when he needed you in the garden, and you denied him three times in his night of greatest need."

Then Luke the evangelist spoke, "You must leave. You have not been found worthy of the kingdom of God."

The man's head bowed sadly for a moment before a spark lit his face. "My life has been recorded correctly. I am guilty as charged. Yet I know there is a place for me in this blessed kingdom. Abraham, David, and Peter will plead my cause because they know of the weakness of people and the mercy of God. You, blessed physician, will open the gates to me because you have written of God's great love for the likes of me. Don't you recognize me? I am the lost sheep that the Good Shepherd carried home. I am your younger, prodigal brother."

And the gates opened and Luke embraced the sinner.

(Taken from *Speaking in Stories* by William B. White, copyright © 1982, Augsburg Publishing House. Reprinted by permission of Augsburg Fortress.)

A Prayer

And lead us not into temptation, but deliver us from the evil one means,

By ourselves we are too weak
to hold our own even for a moment.

And our sworn enemies—
   the devil, the world, and our own flesh—
never stop attacking us.

And so, Lord,
uphold us and make us strong
   with the strength of your Holy Spirit,
so that we may not go down to defeat
   in this spiritual struggle,
but may firmly resist our enemies
   until we finally win the complete victory.

Heidelberg Catechism, Answer 127

THINK ABOUT IT . . .
Are you holding back from publicly professing your faith because you think you're not good enough for Jesus?

LESSON 12

Dear Mr. Howell,

I know the assignment was to write a letter to our parents. I couldn't think of anything to write. I hope you don't mind, but I want to write about Katie. She's a real friend. I bet you wonder why that is important. OK, this is why.

Last fall when school started, I was really feeling terrible. I mean I felt sick. I didn't have any friends. My parents were constantly fighting. Every time I went to bed I first got all my clothes out and ready for school. I wanted to get out of the house in the morning so I wouldn't have to hear Mom and Dad fighting again. I almost hated both of them. I would usually come to school and sit on the floor by my locker. I didn't want to talk to anybody, look at anybody, or be with anybody.

In the fall it was dark in the halls before the janitor put the lights on. I could hear some kids talk about me when they walked by or when I sat in the rooms. They'd say things like "She's so stuck-up; she just looks sick."

But this one girl—Katie—was different. I can't even remember when I first started talking to her. I just remember that every morning she was the next person in school, right after me. She would just walk by and say hi with this big smile. I never said anything back. But Katie just kept on saying "hi."

One day she put her books in her locker and came back and sat down next to me. She asked me about my family and stuff. Like a jerk I started talking about my dad and mom and all our problems. And she would just say, "Oh, no kidding? I can see that would be really rough."

I remember one other thing about Katie; she had lots of friends herself. Whenever the kids would go by, they would say "hi" to Katie and ask her to come along. But she just sat there by me.

Katie would look where I was at noon and sit next to me for lunch. Around Christmas she had a party at her house and asked me to come. I couldn't believe it.

But the big thing is that at the beginning of the year I was really mad at God. I wouldn't see how God could let me live in a home like I did. I was mad at everybody, I guess, even Katie. I remember thinking that she was a big hypocrite when I first heard her say hi to me. But she never stopped doing it. And she didn't care what her friends thought. She just always talked to me.

I don't remember when this started, but I think it was when I asked her why she was so happy all the time. And she just said something like, "Because I love Jesus. He's my friend. He died for me and I'm just glad I know him."

What Katie said wasn't anything preachy. You could tell she meant it. I guess it meant the most when I went to Katie's house one day after school. There was nobody home. She told me that her dad worked until 8:00 every night but that he never complained about it.

She said her mom had died a couple of years before, so all the kids had to help out a lot at home. "Mom's with Jesus because she really loved him," Katie said. "Dad just says 'God will provide.'"

And that's why I've changed, Mr. Howell. I became a Christian too. It all started with Katie's smile. She had lots of friends, but she wanted to talk to me.

I hope you don't mind that I changed the assignment a little, but Katie is real. I just wanted to write about her.

Sincerely,
Linda

Go for It!

Matthew 28:16–20

¹⁶Then the eleven disciples went to Galilee, to the mountain where Jesus had told them to go. ¹⁷When they saw him, they worshiped him; but some doubted. ¹⁸Then Jesus came to them and said, "All authority in heaven and on earth has been given to me. ¹⁹Therefore go and make disciples of all nations, baptizing them in the name of the Father and of the Son and of the Holy Spirit, ²⁰and teaching them to obey everything I have commanded you. And surely I am with you always, to the very end of the age."

Discuss/Decide

1. Underline three things Jesus says all disciples should do. What kind of attitude do you think we should have about doing these things?

2. Circle the phrases that explain how we will be able to do these things.

3. If Jesus were talking to you right now, commissioning you to be his witness, what might he say? Try writing an up-to-date and personal "great commission" in the space below:

4. Read Acts 4:1–21, which describes one of Peter and John's first attempts to carry out the Great Commission. Write two things we can learn about witnessing from their experience:

5. Find a verse in Acts 4:1–21 that clearly tells what witnessing is.

You Can Do It!

Christians can witness just about anytime and anywhere. For each place described below, use your imagination to think of a "witnessing opportunity"—a realistic way to show or tell someone that you're a Christian.

1. *place:* **lunchroom at school**
witnessing opportunity:

2. *place:* **on the school bus**
witnessing opportunity:

3. *place:* **halfway around the world**
witnessing opportunity:

4. *place:* **in the hall after a big science test**
witnessing opportunity:

5. *place:* **at home**
witnessing opportunity:

6. *place:* **at a school sporting event**
witnessing opportunity:

7. *place:* **at a party**
   witnessing opportunity:

8. *place:* **(your choice)**
   witnessing opportunity:

P E R S O N A L

Talking about your personal relationship to Jesus can help another person come to Jesus. Katie's talk with Linda is a good example of this.

What would you say to someone else about your relationship to Jesus? Think about this; then jot down a few of your thoughts about what Jesus means to you.

_____
_____
_____
_____
_____
_____
_____
_____

If you wish, share your thoughts with the class.

LESSON 1: Lord, Call Our Names

MEMORY WORK

"Come to me, all you who are weary and burdened, and I will give you rest. Take my yoke upon you and learn from me, for I am gentle and humble in heart, and you will find rest for your souls. For my yoke is easy and my burden is light."

Matthew 11:28–30

FROM MONDAY TO SATURDAY

MONDAY
Read Matthew 4:18–22. Jesus simply says, "Come, follow me." Why did the men in this passage follow Jesus so readily?

TUESDAY
Read Matthew 4:23–25. Why did the crowds follow Jesus?

WEDNESDAY
Read Matthew 8:18–22. What is Jesus telling the teacher and the disciple about what it means to follow him?

THURSDAY
Read Luke 5:1–11. For what purpose did Jesus call these fishermen to follow him?

FRIDAY
Read John 21:15–22. Why does Jesus ask Peter, who was already a disciple, to follow him *again*?

SATURDAY
Read John 8:12–18. What reason does Jesus give here for why people should follow him?

 **TALK ABOUT IT . . .**
Ask your mom or dad this week's question: If Jesus appeared in person tomorrow, where do you think you would find him? What do your parents think? Why? Would you and your parents be ready to follow him as eagerly as Matthew did?

LESSON 2: LORD, GIVE US FAITH

MEMORY WORK

"So do not worry, saying, 'What shall we eat?' or 'What shall we drink?' or 'What shall we wear?' For the pagans run after all these things, and your heavenly Father knows that you need them. But seek first his kingdom and his righteousness, and all these things will be given to you as well."

Matthew 6:31–33

FROM MONDAY TO SATURDAY

MONDAY
Read Matthew 6:25–34. What do you worry about? What is Jesus' advice for worriers?

TUESDAY
Read Matthew 8:5–13. Why did Jesus say this man had "such great faith"?

WEDNESDAY
Read Matthew 15:21–28. What is peculiar about this woman's faith?

THURSDAY
Read James 5:13–18. What does prayer have to do with faith?

FRIDAY
Read Hebrews 11:1–6. What is faith?

SATURDAY
Read Genesis 22:1–18. What pleased the Lord the most about Abraham's sacrifice?

 **TALK ABOUT IT . . .**
Ask your dad or mom what he or she fears or worries about most. How does faith in Jesus help him or her handle fear and worry?

Lesson 3: LORD, HELP US LISTEN

MEMORY WORK

"For everyone who asks receives; he who seeks finds; and to him who knocks, the door will be opened."

Matthew 7:8

FROM MONDAY TO SATURDAY

MONDAY
Read John 12:1–8. In this record of the visit to Mary and Martha, who objects to Mary's act? Why?

TUESDAY
Read Matthew 26:36–46. What did Jesus wish for his disciples?

WEDNESDAY
Read Matthew 5:1–12. What is Jesus' purpose in having the disciples sit down and listen?

THURSDAY
Read Mark 9:33–37. Why were the disciples arguing? What was Jesus' answer?

FRIDAY
Read John 17:6–19. What does Jesus teach us about his relationship to his disciples?

SATURDAY
Read John 17:20–26. What is Jesus' prayer for all believers?

 **THINK ABOUT IT . . .**
There are many ways, besides reading the Bible, in which you can "listen" to Jesus and be in touch with him. Name some ways that you can use; then set aside a time to use one approach in your quiet time this week.

LESSON 4: LORD, TEACH US TO PRAY

MEMORY WORK

Our Father in heaven,
hallowed be your name,
your kingdom come,
your will be done
    on earth as it is in heaven.
Give us today our daily bread.
Forgive us our debts,
    as we also have forgiven our
        debtors.
And lead us not into temptation,
    but deliver us from the evil one.
For yours is the kingdom
    and the power
    and the glory forever.
                     Amen.

              The Lord's Prayer

FROM MONDAY TO SATURDAY

MONDAY
Read Matthew 26:36–46. What does Jesus teach you about prayer in these verses?

TUESDAY
Read Luke 11:1–13. What does Jesus' story about the friend teach you about prayer? How is that different from the "vain repetitions" he warns against in the lesson you had in class?

WEDNESDAY
Read Luke 18:1–8. What is the relationship between prayer and faith?

THURSDAY
Read Luke 18:9–14. What is the difference between the two prayers being offered in these verses? What lesson can you learn from this story?

FRIDAY
Read John 17:20–26. Prayer is fellowship with God. What can you tell about the relationship Jesus has to his Father?

SATURDAY
Read Philippians 4:4–9. What is the benefit of prayer?

 **THINK ABOUT IT . . .**
All of the references in the Lord's Prayer are plural: *we* and *our* rather than *I* or *mine*. Why do you think Jesus gave us this model?

LESSON 5: LORD, HELP US TO CARE

MEMORY WORK

"For I was hungry and you gave me something to eat, I was thirsty and you gave me something to drink, I was a stranger and you invited me in, I needed clothes and you clothed me, I was sick and you looked after me, I was in prison and you came to visit me."

Matthew 25:35–36

FROM MONDAY TO SATURDAY

MONDAY
Read Mark 8:1–21. What didn't the disciples understand?

TUESDAY
Read Matthew 20:29–34. What is the difference between Jesus and the crowd?

WEDNESDAY
Read Mark 9:33–37. What is the difference between the actions of Jesus and the actions of his disciples?

THURSDAY
Read Luke 15:11–24. What does the father's action toward his returning son tell us about God?

FRIDAY
Read 2 Corinthians 1:3–7. For what purpose does Christ comfort us?

SATURDAY
Read Matthew 25:31–46. What really separates the "sheep" from the "goats"?

 **THINK ABOUT IT . . .**

How old does a person have to be to have empathy and show compassion for someone else? Is there an age limit on caring? Here's a list of ways *you* might be able to reach out and show concern for someone:
- Get together with some friends and have a scavenger hunt for groceries you can donate to a church food bank.
- Donate some of your clothes to a clothing bank for needy people.
- Do chores for neighbors or church members who are unable to do the jobs themselves.
- Volunteer to be a tutor for a student who is having difficulty in school.
- Read to or visit someone in a nursing home who would like company.

LESSON 6: LORD, MAKE US MORE LIKE YOU

MEMORY WORK

" 'Love the Lord with all your heart and with all your soul and with all your mind.' This is the first and greatest commandment. And the second is like it: 'Love your neighbor as yourself.' All the Law and the Prophets hang on these two commandments."

Matthew 22:37–40

FROM MONDAY TO SATURDAY

MONDAY
Read Acts 4:13–20. How could the people tell that Peter and John had been "with Jesus"?

TUESDAY
Read 1 Peter 2:9–12. What will pagans do when they see Christians living for Jesus?

WEDNESDAY
Read 2 Corinthians 2:14–17. What does it mean to be the "fragrance" of Christ?

THURSDAY
Read Ephesians 3:14–19. How does Paul want the Christians in these verses to be filled?

FRIDAY
Read Isaiah 6:1–7. What picture do you get of God's holiness?

SATURDAY
Read Titus 2:9–14. What does God's grace do in our lives? Why did Jesus die?

 **THINK ABOUT IT . . .**
If you were arrested for being a disciple of Christ, would there be enough evidence to convict you?

LESSON 7: LORD, MAKE US FORGIVING

MEMORY WORK

Be kind and compassionate to one another, forgiving each other, just as in Christ God forgave you.

Ephesians 4:32

FROM MONDAY TO SATURDAY

MONDAY
Read Matthew 9:1–8. What does Jesus teach here about forgiveness?

TUESDAY
Read Mark 11:20–25. What must come *before* Christ's forgiveness?

WEDNESDAY
Read Luke 17:1–4. Is it harder to warn or to forgive?

THURSDAY
Read Luke 23:32–43. What do you learn about Jesus' forgiveness on the cross?

FRIDAY
Read John 20:19–23. What did Jesus pass on to his disciples?

SATURDAY
Read 2 Corinthians 2:5–11. What is Paul's advice? What does the phrase "if there was anything to forgive" suggest about our forgiving?

 **THINK ABOUT IT . . .**
When you talk to others, which of the following seems the easiest to do? The hardest? What does Jesus ask his disciples to do?
- warn, threaten
- forgive
- praise, thank
- encourage
- lie, deceive
- compliment
- confess to
- sympathize with
- cheer, make laugh
- put down, mock

LESSON 8: LORD, DISCIPLINE OUR LIVES

MEMORY WORK

Do you not know that in a race all the runners run, but only one gets the prize? Run in such a way as to get the prize. Everyone who competes in the games goes into strict training. They do it to get a crown that will not last; but we do it to get a crown that will last forever.

1 Corinthians 9:24–25

FROM MONDAY TO SATURDAY

MONDAY
Read Matthew 6:19–24. Why can't we seek two treasures?

TUESDAY
Read Philippians 3:17–21. What is the end of people who are controlled by Christ? Who is the god for those who aren't?

WEDNESDAY
Read Luke 8:11–15. What does the self-discipline of reading the Bible have to do with following Jesus?

THURSDAY
Read 1 John 3:16–24. How does Jesus command us to live in relationship to him? To each other?

FRIDAY
Read 2 Timothy 3:1–5. What are the results of people being "lovers of themselves"?

SATURDAY
Read Jude 17–23. What does a Christian disciple have to do?

 **THINK ABOUT IT . . .**
Webster's Ninth New Collegiate Dictionary defines the verb *discipline* in three different ways: (1) to punish or penalize; (2) to train or develop by instruction and exercise; and (3) to bring under control or impose order upon. Which definition fits the theme of lesson 8 best? How has lesson 8 affected the way you think about your own life as a disciple of Jesus?

LESSON 9: LORD, GIVE US COURAGE

MEMORY WORK

"If anyone would come after me, he must deny himself and take up his cross and follow me."

Matthew 16:24

FROM MONDAY TO SATURDAY

MONDAY
Read Isaiah 53. What kinds of suffering did Jesus endure for us? What was his reaction to suffering?

TUESDAY
Read 1 Peter 4:12–19. Christians can expect some suffering. What should our attitude toward suffering be?

WEDNESDAY
Read Acts 4:1–22. How did Peter and John respond to the threats of the religious leaders?

THURSDAY
Read Acts 6:8–15 and 7:54–60. In what ways was Stephen like Jesus?

FRIDAY
Read 2 Corinthians 11:21b–33. Mention some of the things that Paul suffered because he was a follower of Jesus.

SATURDAY
Read Romans 5:1–5. What was Paul's attitude toward suffering? What benefits can suffering bring?

 **TALK ABOUT IT . . .**
Talk to your dad or mom about a time when he or she experienced trouble or suffering of some kind. How did God help during that sad time?

LESSON 10: LORD, ACCEPT OUR THANKS

MEMORY WORK

You are my God, and I will give you thanks;
   you are my God, and I will exalt you.
Give thanks to the LORD, for he is good;
   his love endures forever.

Psalm 118:28–29

FROM MONDAY TO SATURDAY

MONDAY
Read Psalm 27:1–6. What does the psalmist want to do in the temple?

TUESDAY
Read Luke 7:36–50. What did Jesus notice about this woman's gift?

WEDNESDAY
Read Colossians 2:1–7. What does "overflowing with thankfulness" mean?

THURSDAY
Read 1 Thessalonians 5:12–22. How would giving thanks in "all circumstances" help us?

FRIDAY
Read Psalm 118:15–29. What "flavor" does thanking have here?

SATURDAY
Read Nehemiah 12:31–47. What can you discover in this passage about what *group* thanks should be like?

 **THINK ABOUT IT . . .**
In lesson 10 you learned about Mary's expensive gift, accepted by Jesus as a symbol of her love and gratitude to him. As a disciple of Jesus, what specific acts of thanks could you offer with your own money, time, talents, and creativity? Write down at least three.

LESSON 11: LORD, HELP US GROW

MEMORY WORK

If we confess our sins, he is faithful and just and will forgive us our sins and purify us from all unrighteousness.

1 John 1:9

FROM MONDAY TO SATURDAY

Learn more about Peter from his experiences recorded in the book of Acts. Tell how each of the following passages shows Peter's growing faith in Jesus Christ.

MONDAY
Read Acts 2:1–15, 36–41.

TUESDAY
Read Acts 3:1–16.

WEDNESDAY
Read Acts 4:1–22.

THURSDAY
Read Acts 5:17–33.

FRIDAY
Read Acts 11:1–18.

SATURDAY
Read Acts 12:1–19.

 **TALK ABOUT IT . . .**
Have you already publicly professed your faith in Christ? Are you thinking about doing it? How do you know if you're ready? Talk it over with your mom, dad, or pastor.

LESSON 12: LORD, HELP US WITNESS

Directions
You'll need a Bible, a pen or pencil, your student book, and a quiet place for thinking. Use everything you've learned about discipleship to answer the questions on this page. (Use the back side of this page, if necessary.) Return the completed page to your teacher next week.

1. Select one passage that you memorized during the past few weeks. Write it out from memory below; then explain how the passage can help you become a better disciple of Jesus. (If you didn't memorize any passages, pick one passage we studied and tell how it can help you be a disciple.)

2. It's easy to forget what you learned weeks ago, so take a few minutes to page through your student book. Pick one lesson or part of a lesson that you enjoyed. Tell why you liked it and what it taught you about being a disciple of Jesus.

3. Think some more about what you learned in this course. Then complete the following statement in 100 words or more:

   In this course, I have learned that following Jesus means . . .

4. In what way, if any, has this course on discipleship affected how you think about Jesus? About yourself?

5. In what way, if any, has this course on discipleship affected your daily life? Explain.